FEELINGS IN ART

Clare Gogerty

Artwork: Celia Chester

CHERRYTREE BOOKS

A Cherrytree book

Designed and reproduced by Touchstone Publishing Ltd

Copyright this edition © Evans Brothers Ltd 2003
Published by Cherrytree Press Ltd
327 High Street
Slough Berks SL1 1TX

First published in 1994
First paperback edition published 2003

Designer: David Armitage
Cover designer: Simon Borrough

Cover picture: *The Scream*, Edvard Munch

British Library Cataloguing in Publication Data
Gogerty, Clare
        Feelings in Art. – (In Art Series)
        I. Title II. Series
        707

        ISBN 1 84234 178 2

Printed in China through Colorcraft Ltd., Hong Kong

Contents

In every chapter of this book you will find a number of coloured panels. Each one has a symbol at the top to tell you what type of panel it is.

Activity panel Ideas for projects that will give you an insight into the techniques of the artists in this book. Try your hand at painting, sculpting and crafts.

Information panel Detailed explanations of particular aspects of the text, or in-depth information on an artist or work of art.

Look and See panel Suggestions for some close observation, using this book, the library, art galleries, and the art and architecture in your area.

1 Happiness

Moving pictures

Do you find that sometimes your mood changes when you look at a painting? Some paintings are so sad they make us feel sad. Others are such happy subjects that they fill us with joy and pleasure.

Not all works of art do this. Some simply record an event, person or place. Others are purely for decoration. This means that they are highly patterned and are painted in attractive colours. They are pleasant to look at but do not move us emotionally.

Happy times

There are different types of happiness. There is the hilarious, thigh-slapping, gutsy, good-time sort of happiness we share with friends. Then there is the peaceful, absorbing sort of contentment we feel when we are alone.

Different artists choose to paint different kinds of happiness. The methods and techniques they use, however, are much the same. The most effective way to show a feeling is with colour. Artists vary the colours they use depending on what kind of mood they want to create. For a happy mood they use colours such as yellow, red, orange, bright blue and bright green. Sad paintings have dark colours: grey, black, brown, for example.

▼ *When you look at this mask does it make you smile? It is hard to keep a straight face when someone else is laughing. The artist knew this and exaggerated the expression to increase the effect. The mask was designed for use in the Japanese Theatre of Kyogen.*

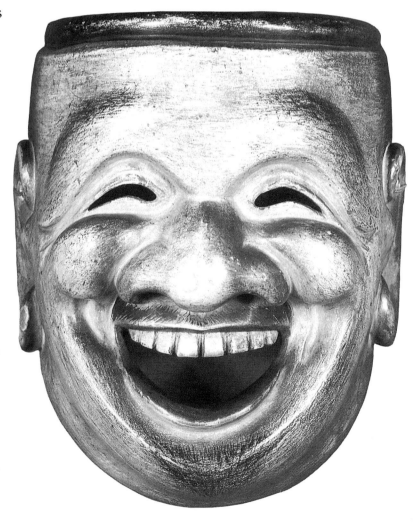

▲ *Matisse, who painted this picture, tried to show feelings through the movement of the body. Look at how the figures leap and stretch and dance. What do you think they are feeling? There are only three major colours in this picture: bright blue, bright green and terracotta. They are all cheerful colours. What colours would you use to paint a gloomy picture?*
[La Danse, *Henri Matisse*]

Bright colours lift the mood of the painting and of the person looking at it. Sometimes a colour can affect a person's mood because it reminds them of something else. A bright blue may remind you of a summer sky; a jolly yellow of the sun; a pretty pink of a favourite flower or the strawberry ice-cream you loved when you were a child.

One artist who used this emotional power of colour very effectively was the French painter and sculptor Henri Matisse.

Happy colours

Matisse believed that when an artist paints, he should use a colour that matches his mood. Matisse's own pictures are full of brilliant colours: bright blue, blue-green emerald, warm terracotta, sunny yellow. These colours all suggest happiness and good, positive feelings.

Matisse never painted gloomy things. Troubling or depressing subjects did not interest him – he thought that a piece of art should soothe and calm. He compared one of his paintings to a good armchair; somewhere to rest and feel comfortable.

Matisse was the leader of a group of artists called the Fauves. Other Fauves included André Derain and Raoul Dufy. Fauves is a French word meaning 'wild beasts' or 'savages'. The artists were given this name because people were astonished by their wild use of bright colours. Instead of modelling with carefully shaded, realistic colours, the Fauves painted in large, flat areas of one colour. These colours were often unexpected. Matisse painted a portrait of his wife with a green nose and a yellow cheek, for example.

Matisse and the Fauves liked to keep their pictures simple. As well as bright colours, they used strong, clear outlines. They wanted as many people as possible to be moved to pleasure by their work, and thought that this simple, direct method was the most effective way to do it.

Put on a happy face

Another way to make people smile is to paint a happy face. Laughter and cheerfulness are infectious – it is hard to keep a

Dance, dance, dance

One of the best ways to express, and experience, happiness is by dancing. Pictures of dancing figures, such as the one by Henri Matisse on page 5, embody the feeling of joy that comes from moving to music.

Artists have enjoyed painting the excitement of dance since ancient times. There are pictures of dancers on walls of tombs and on vases from ancient Greece. Dancing figures have also always been popular subjects with Japanese printmakers.

In more recent times, many French artists painted dancers. Henri Toulouse-Lautrec visited music halls in Paris, particularly the Folies-Bergère, and sketched the dancers there. He used some of these sketches in the posters he designed to advertise dance events. Auguste Renoir liked to go to the open-air dances in Paris and paint the couples dancing outside in the sunshine and moonlight.

straight face when someone is grinning at you.

Frans Hals, a Dutch painter who lived 300 years ago, painted a famous picture that is popularly known as *The Laughing Cavalier*. (In fact, the subject is not laughing at all and his expression is sometimes described as a smirk, or disdainful half smile.) Like many of Hals's other portraits, this picture captures one fleeting facial expression. This is hard for any artist to do because the face is constantly moving. Hals managed it by using many small, dashing brushstrokes, as if he were making a quick sketch.

Frans Hals looked at what he was painting very carefully. He studied how the parts of a person's face fit together and what happens to it when it moves. Study your own face and watch how it changes. Stand in front of the mirror and smile at your reflection. Look at what has happened to your face. The eyes are now smaller and a different shape, the cheeks have moved upwards, the mouth has stretched sideways, and lines have formed around the eyes.

When an artist paints a happy person, he has to include all these things. Some artists, especially cartoonists and designers of masks, exaggerate some of them so that the expression is easier to see and to understand.

▶ *The man in this picture looks as though he is about to burst out laughing. Although his mouth is straight, his eyes are smiling, and the way he is standing is jolly and good natured. This expression is very subtle but the artist has managed to capture it. Look at the complicated clothes the man is wearing. Notice how the artist has used different sorts of brushstrokes for different sorts of fabric.* [The Laughing Cavalier, *Frans Hals*]

Many adverts on television and in magazines show happy, smiling people. The people in the pictures are always beautiful, successful and surrounded by desirable things. How do they make you feel? If you feel envious, the advertisement has worked. The advertisers hope that you will buy what is being advertised to make your life like those of the people in the ads.

Domestic happiness

Some of the best and happiest times in our lives are spent doing quite ordinary things. During the nineteenth century, these activities were popular subjects with artists. They wanted to share their enjoyment of everyday pleasures with other people.

One American painter, Mary Cassatt, brilliantly captured the joys of life at home. Her pictures show people peacefully doing simple things. A baby is bathed by his mother, a grandmother reads to her grandchildren, a woman drinks a cup of tea alone and in perfect contentment. In her pictures, Mary Cassatt created an ideal world. Each one is filled with light, fresh colours, her figures are always fashionably dressed and no one ever argues or is sad.

Sometimes painters make scenes like these look sugary and sentimental, as though their subjects did not have to put up with the realities of everyday life. Look at happy pictures with a critical eye. Do you think they are realistic? Do they tell the truth about life?

▲ *This picture shows a moment of contentment. The woman drinking tea is alone but perfectly happy. She is smiling to herself with pleasure. The whole picture has a happy, summery feeling. To create this feeling the artist has used fresh, delicate colours and sketchy brushwork.* [The Cup of Tea, *Mary Cassatt*]

Happy and sad landscapes

The weather can change our moods. Cloudy, rainy days can make us feel sad and depressed but hot, sunny days may cheer us up. This has a lot to do with colour. When it is cold and wet, the sky turns grey and there is not much light. When it is hot and sunny, the colours are brighter and clearer. Remember the way colour affects moods when you paint landscapes.

What you need
- watercolour paints
- water
- paper
- paintbrush

What you do

1 Find a view that you will enjoy painting. It doesn't have to be a beach scene like the one shown here. It could be the view from your bedroom window, or you could paint your garden, if you have one.

2 Wait until the sun shines and then spend a few minutes looking at the scene in front of you. Look at the shapes of the clouds (if there are any). What colours can you see?

3 It is difficult to make corrections with watercolour paint. If you paint over what you have already painted, you may end up with dirty brown smudges. Mix your colours carefully before painting. If it is a sunny day, you will need bright colours, such as yellow and pink and sky blue. For dark areas, such as shadows, mix a bright colour in with your dark colour to make the darker patches look warmer.

4 Now wait for a cold, rainy day and paint the same scene. You will have to use darker colours, such as grey, navy blue and green, to create a cold picture that makes the viewer shiver. Notice how the light is different and how this changes all the colours. Look at the shadows. On a sunny day, they are clear and sharp. What happens to them when it is cloudy?

2 Anger

Feeling angry

Anger is a feeling that sweeps over us when something is wrong. It affects the way we think and the way we move. It can grip us in a tense, unhappy way and bring about feelings of hatred and disgust. It isn't necessarily a bad thing, however. By feeling angry, we can be prompted to take action to change things. For example, horrifying scenes on television of war or starvation, can make us angry that such things are allowed to happen. As a result, we may try to change what we have seen.

Anger can also be a private pain. We feel it when we are wrongly accused of something, or when we disagree strongly with someone else's point of view.

When an artist paints a picture of anger, he or she approaches it very differently from a picture of happiness. The colours are different, darker and more intense; the figures look disturbed and violent; often there is a lot of movement to create a feeling of agitation and distress.

Angry artists

Imagine you were a soldier who fought in the trenches in World War I. Every day you saw people killed or maimed and only just escaped injury yourself. Afterwards, nothing

▲ This Japanese print shows an actor playing the part of a character in a play. He is clearly very angry. See how his face is creased with rage.
[Otani Oniji as Eitoku, Tokhusai Sharaku]

10

Photomontage

The artist John Heartfield made pictures by gluing different photographs on to paper. He found the photographs in all kinds of places. Some were from newspapers, some from magazines, some from friends' photograph collections. This method of creating a picture is called photomontage.

Heartfield's skill was in deciding which pictures to cut out and where to place them. He often made surprising choices, placing unlikely things side by side.

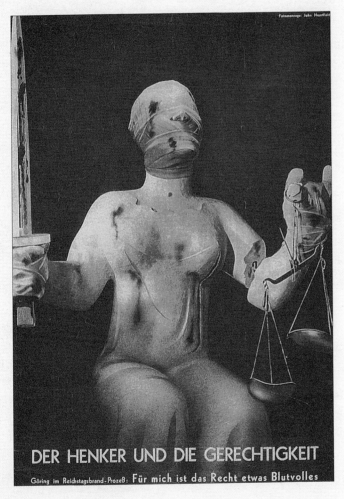

DER HENKER UND DIE GERECHTIGKEIT

Göring im Reichstagsbrand-Prozeß: Für mich ist das Recht etwas Blutvolles

▲ *This picture was created out of anger. John Heartfield was outraged by the fact that justice no longer existed in Hitler's Germany. The figure of Justice is shown injured, gagged by her bandages and powerless. It is a simple but strong image.*
[Justica, *John Heartfield*]

in your country seems to be any different. All the suffering and misery was for nothing.

This was the experience of Otto Dix and several other artists in Germany. After the war, they were so sickened and angry that they wanted everyone else to know what had gone on. They wanted to prevent the same thing happening again.

Dix fought in the front line during the war. When it was over he made paintings and etchings of what he had seen: war invalids with terrible mutilations and awful artificial limbs. He saw rich people living comfortable, wasteful lives whilst the poor people who had fought were living in hardship.

Like Dix, the artist George Grosz had fought in the war. His paintings powerfully expose the injustices and greed that he saw in Berlin. They show grotesque men and women concerned only with their own pleasure. He painted officials who had made money from the war. He showed them so absorbed in their wealth that they did not notice or care about the hardship all around them.

Angry posters

Grosz worked closely with another artist and war veteran called John Heartfield. Both men were hostile to the Nazi party and its leader Adolf Hitler, who rose to power in Germany during the 1930s. Hitler believed that Germany needed a strong leadership. Eventually, he banned all other political parties except his own and ruled Germany by terror and force.

The more popular Hitler became, the more angry Heartfield grew. He wanted people to realize how evil and destructive Nazism was. He tried to communicate his feelings by producing posters made in a technique called photomontage (see page 11). These images are very powerful: for example, in one picture a dove – the symbol of peace – is shown impaled on a bayonet.

▲ *This picture shows a famous boxing match between Jack Dempsey and Luis Firpo. Firpo has just knocked Dempsey out of the ring. Firpo's face is controlled and still, he is disguising the anger and aggression he feels. Look at the faces of the spectators. Can you work out what each one is feeling?*
[Dempsey and Firpo, *George Bellows*]

▼ *This is a scene from the New Testament when Jesus drives out the money changers from the temple. He was very angry to find trading going on inside God's house. The artist has shown Jesus' anger through the movement of his body. His arm is raised as if to hit someone. Look at how the people are recoiling from him in fear.* [Christ Driving the Money Changers from the Temple (detail), *El Greco*]

Many of Heartfield's photomontages are satirical. This means that they show up the foolishness of something by poking fun at it. One called *Berlin Dialect*, for example, shows a pair of ears stuck on to each side of a man's bottom. What do you think this means?

Unfortunately, all these angry, biting pictures did not stop Hitler coming to power. When he ruled Germany he persecuted and exiled the artists who had opposed him.

Often groups of people form organizations to protest against something they feel angry about. They may feel strongly about what is happening to the environment, or about a war that is taking place. Often they produce posters to tell people about these things. See if you can find any. Look at their design. Do they make you feel angry, too? Is there something that makes *you* angry? Why not design a poster to tell people about it.

Goya

Not many artists painted angry pictures about the futility of war before these artists. This was because, until modern times, most artists were paid to paint pictures by rich and important people who wanted only heroic, optimistic paintings.

Francisco José de Goya, a Spanish artist who died in 1828, was an exception. One of his paintings *The Third of May 1808* shows the horrors and brutality of the invasion of Spain by Napoleon Bonaparte. He also made a series of engravings called *The Disasters of War* that shows the sufferings of individuals during wartime.

Angry faces

Both our bodies and our faces change when we are angry. Try and draw what your face looks like when you are in a really angry mood.

What you need
- black felt-tip pen or charcoal
- paper
- mirror

What you do
1 Sit in front of the mirror and pull angry faces. Narrow your eyes and clench your teeth. Put your chin out and flare your nostrils. Screw your face up with rage.
2 Make a cartoon drawing of each face you pull. Use a black felt-tip pen or a piece of charcoal and draw simple lines. Try to capture the expression in just a few lines by exaggerating what you see. Notice how the shape of the eyes changes and the line of the mouth. Draw your cartoon quickly, don't spend ages thinking about it.

Ways of expressing anger

One way artists express anger is by using very strong images. Another is by painting figures in an exaggerated, distorted way. An artist called El Greco, who painted in Spain during the sixteenth century, was a master at using the body to show feelings. Unlike the later German artists though, he did not paint life around him, he painted pictures of stories from the Bible. His pictures contain highly-charged feelings of love and anger. He created these feelings by stretching his figures, and twisting them.

El Greco used unusual, harsh colour combinations in his pictures, such as blue and lemon. These colours together create an unsettling effect; they seem to 'fight' each other. Another colour combination that has this effect is red and green. By using these colours together, an artist can create disturbing, angry feelings.

Mr Angry

An American called David Lynch created a cartoon character called the Angriest Dog in the World. This dog is so angry he can't move. Every week in the cartoon he hasn't changed his position. His anger has made him completely rigid.

Think of other angry body positions and make drawings of them.

What you need
• pastels   • paper

What you do

1 Either get together with a friend or stand in front of a full-length mirror and make different angry postures and pull angry faces. For example: stand with your feet together and your arms crossed, shut your mouth tightly and crossly; clench your fist and shake it in the air; scowl. How do you feel when you are making these angry gestures?

2 Now draw each of these postures. Exaggerate them a little to make them seem even angrier. Draw sharp, slashing lines as you sketch to emphasize the feelings of anger.

3 Try using both of these figures to create a scene which shows people arguing.

3 Grief

Unhappy times

There are times in our lives when we feel terribly unhappy. Sometimes this is because something awful has happened to us, or we have done something we regret. At other times we feel unhappy for another person. This person may be ill or distressed, or may even have died.

The name given to this feeling is grief. Grief is a very strong feeling. It can so overpower people that they feel nothing else. The world looks black and without hope. It is especially strong when someone close to us dies. It is hard to cope with the idea that the loved one has gone away and won't come back.

Many artists have painted feelings of grief. These pictures can move us so much that we share their pain. When people are unhappy they look different from when they are happy. The expressions on their faces change. They move their bodies in a different way. When artists paint grieving people they have to show these differences.

Picasso's broken faces

The Spanish artist Pablo Picasso painted many pictures of unhappy people. His people don't look like anyone you might see on the street. Their faces look as though they have been smashed to pieces and put back together the wrong way.

▲ *Auguste Rodin, who sculpted this head in bronze, has managed to capture one fleeting expression powerfully. We can only imagine why this girl is crying, but we can understand how she is feeling. Look at the shape of her mouth and the way her eyes have narrowed. [Head of a Girl Crying, Auguste Rodin]*

When we look at Picasso's crumpled, fractured faces, we know straight away that something is wrong. By distorting the face and exaggerating the expression, he makes the sadness of the subject apparent immediately.

Picasso also used unusual colours to match the mood of the person he was painting.

He would paint a face in vivid yellow and vivid green, for example. These are not calm, peaceful colours; they are violent and angry. They make the painting even more confused and distressed.

These 'broken-up' paintings are called Cubist paintings (see page 18). In his Cubist pictures, Picasso

▶ *Pablo Picasso, who painted this picture, has distorted the woman's face to convey a feeling of great unhappiness. The jagged lines, violent colours and jumble of features and hands is both disturbing and distressing.* [Woman Weeping (1937), *Pablo Picasso*]

Cubism

Some artists try to paint what they see as accurately as possible. They want their pictures to look realistic. Others interpret what they see. They do not just paint what is in front of them; they look for other things, too.

Pablo Picasso and a French artist called Georges Braque invented a way of painting called Cubism. When they looked at an object, a bowl of fruit for example, they saw a set of different shapes – spheres, columns, cones and cubes. As they painted, they did not just paint one side of these shapes, but all of the sides. They broke up what they painted into many different surfaces, creating a variety of patterns and textures.

wanted to show several different aspects of the same person or object at the same time. Instead of painting just what was in front of him, he painted what was hidden as well. For example, a face is shown in profile (from the side) but we can see both eyes.

Body language

As well as distorting facial expressions to show feelings of grief, artists use the shape and movement of the body. If you study the way someone

▲ *The dead men have been executed for murder at the order of the judge shown in the background. Many people, including the painter, believed they were innocent. The three standing men were among those who passed judgement against the men. What feelings do their facial expressions and the flowers they carry convey? What do you think the artist felt about these men?* [The Passion of Sacco and Vanzetti, *Ben Shahn*]

Photographs in newspapers often show terrible scenes of suffering and grief. Sometimes, these pictures are taken during a war or at the scene of a disaster. Try and find some. Look at the way people move their bodies and how their expressions change when they are unhappy. Do you think that these photographs are as powerful emotionally as the paintings in this chapter, or more so?

sits, stands and moves, you can often get a good idea of what they are thinking. If you see someone who is walking slowly, hands deep in pockets, head bowed, the chances are that he or she is feeling sad or depressed. These gestures that communicate what we are feeling and thinking are called body language.

Body language is useful to artists. By painting or sculpting a figure in a posture that we recognize, for example, holding head in hands and weeping, we know what that figure is feeling.

Tragic figures

Religious books have many stories of grief and suffering in them. Artists throughout history have illustrated these scenes in paintings, books and sculpture. In the fifteenth

The art of death

When people die, their bodies are often buried in a holy place. Sometimes, especially in the past, graves and tombs were decorated with sculpture, paintings and mosaics.

In ancient China, the nobility were buried in large tombs. The walls of these were often decorated with paintings of the dead person's life. The entrances to some were guarded by stone statues of fabulous beasts to keep away the evil spirits. In 209 BC, one Chinese nobleman was buried with 500 clay warriors and 24 clay horses. These were meant to protect him in the afterlife.

In England there is a tradition of nobles having life-size statues lying on the top of their tombs. These statues are of the people buried inside and are called effigies.

Some effigies have two pillows beneath their heads – one for the physical body and one for the soul. Often the statues' feet rest on a stone replica of something that symbolizes their family – a dog, or a castle, or maybe even a porcupine.

Around the sides of these tombs there are often smaller, weeping figures. These 'weepers' are usually replicas of the members of the dead person's family.

In Victorian times, the tombs of the rich became even more extravagant. Some, like the Chinese ones, were big enough to walk inside. They were decorated with life-size marble figures, some of the dead person, others of angels. Westminster Abbey in London is full of marble figures like these.

century in Italy, the Church and some rich patrons paid to have pictures from the Bible painted on the walls of churches and chapels. These pictures are often tragic, and the figures in them show deep, sorrowful feelings. This had rarely been seen before in western art. Artists began to paint freely people who looked as though they really were suffering. Before this, people in pictures seldom showed expression on their faces, and they stood very still and straight.

Many artists have painted the crucifixion of Jesus. Giotto, Michelangelo and others painted pictures of the sad scene in which Jesus is taken down from the cross and is surrounded by his mourning friends and family. These pictures are called pietàs (*pietà* is Italian for 'pity').

Other stories from the Bible were illustrated, too. One artist called Masaccio painted many of them (his real name was Tommaso di Giovanni Guidi; Masaccio was just his nickname). He was most famous for a series of pictures he painted on the walls of the Brancacci Chapel in Florence, Italy. The most

◄ You can tell straight away that something terrible has happened to these people. Look at how the woman is howling with despair and how the man is holding his head in his hands. They are Adam and Eve and have just been thrown out of paradise by God. They are grieving for what they have lost and regretting what they have done. Find the chapter in the Bible that describes this scene and compare what you read with what you see.
[Adam and Eve Banished from Paradise, *Masaccio*]

Unhappy figures

Modelling figures out of clay is easy if you see the body in terms of three-dimensional shapes. Think of the head as a sphere, the trunk of the body as a long cube, the legs and arms as columns. Sometimes it is simpler to make these shapes out of clay first and then join them together. Try making a model of an unhappy person.

What you need
• clay • water • modelling tools

What you do
1 Ask a friend to sit or stand in an unhappy-looking position – with head in hands as though weeping, for example, or with head bowed and arms dangling. Make sure the position is comfortable as they may have to keep still for some time.
2 Bang the clay around a bit to make it soft and workable. Begin to shape the body. Either make it from simple shapes or model it straight out of the lump of clay (as in the picture below), whichever feels easier.
3 Concentrate on getting the feeling of unhappiness across.

Don't worry about details like facial features, or the hair and clothes. Think about how you are going to show unhappiness through the shape of the body.
4 If the clay starts to get dry and difficult to work with, splash a little water over it.
5 If your friend gets stiff, stop so he or she can move around. Remember the position of the body though, so you can carry on sculpting afterwards. Some artists mark the position of the model's feet on the floor with chalk, but you had better check this is OK with an adult first.

famous of them shows the dramatic moment when Adam and Eve were cast out of paradise. Eve is throwing back her head and howling, and Adam is covering his face with shame. By using such expressive body language, Masaccio's figures showed their weighty emotions.

 # **Peace**

Finding peace

Sometimes it is hard to be peaceful. There is so much going on in the world, so many people, so many things to see and do. Quiet times can be hard to find in the middle of all the excitement. It is even harder, of course, in countries where there is a war.

Different people find peace in different places. Some like to lie in the sun relaxing, some like to lose themselves in an activity, some like to meditate, others find peace in the company of friends.

Like other feelings, describing a peaceful scene requires particular techniques.

In a peaceful picture the artist has to keep everything under control. Composition, colour and movement have to be carefully organized. Anything out of place would alter the feeling of the whole painting.

At your leisure

No one understood this technique better than the French painter Georges Seurat. His paintings are calm and untroubled. Several show people peacefully enjoying leisure time out of doors. The atmosphere in these paintings is totally tranquil and, when you look at them, you are filled with a feeling of calm, unhurried pleasure.

◀ *Two of the women in this picture are lost in deep sleep. Another one is looking straight at us. They all look very peaceful and relaxed. Look at all the different sorts of white in the picture. See how many different shades of one colour you can mix with your paints.*
[Dreamers, *Albert Moore*]

▶ *This picture captures the peace and pleasure of a summer Sunday. Everybody is quietly enjoying the sunshine and the water. Many people are lost in their own thoughts. Look at how the picture is painted. Even though there are so many people in a small space, there is no conflict. The scene is so peaceful, you could hear a pin drop.* [Un Dimanche d'été à l'Ile de la Grande Jatte (Sunday Afternoon on the Isle of the Grande Jatte), *Georges Seurat*]

This feeling took a lot of time and a lot of trouble to create. Some of Seurat's paintings took him over a year to paint. One of the reasons for this was that certain paintings were made up of thousands of small brushstrokes. Seurat built up his pictures with small dabs of colour, a technique called Pointillism, which he invented (see information box).

He also took great pains with the composition of each painting. Composition means the way everything fits together. When a picture has been composed properly, it is balanced and easy to 'read'. In paintings of peaceful subjects nothing is out of place or unexpected.

Spots before the eyes

Pointillism, which was invented by Georges Seurat, is a way of painting with dots. Seurat put the paint on to his pictures in small dabs of primary colour. Each dab was the same size and each one was placed at a regular distance from the others. The idea was that instead of mixing the colours on the palette, the eyes of the spectator would mix them in the head. The colours would then stay as bright as when they came out of the tube.

Because everything in a Pointillist painting is broken up into dots, sometimes the pictures appear faint. The lack of strong lines or solid blocks of colours make the images shimmer and fade. Although this is attractive to look at, it wasn't what Seurat intended.

Seurat also painted his figures in a careful, orderly way. They are shown sitting, standing or lying by themselves, very still and very relaxed. Each one is caught up in his or her own thoughts.

Domestic tranquillity

Jan Vermeer, a Dutch artist who lived 200 years before Seurat, also painted calm, solitary people. Unlike Seurat however, who often painted his people out of doors surrounded by other figures, Vermeer's characters are shown inside, often alone, and busy with domestic tasks. They are completely absorbed in these chores, quiet and self-contained, peaceful and content.

To create this calm atmosphere, Vermeer used composition, colour and light very skilfully.

◀ *The woman in this picture is making lace. She is completely absorbed by what she is doing. It can be very peaceful to lose yourself in an activity. The light in the picture is golden and bright, and seems to hold everything in place. Can you work out where it is coming from by looking at the shadows?*
[The Lacemaker, *Jan Vermeer*]

The light in his paintings is strong and steady. Often it enters the scene from the side, throwing dark shadows, but also capturing brilliant highlights. His figures seem to be caught in this light, as though time has stopped at this moment.

Vermeer, again like Seurat, planned each painting's composition very carefully. Before he had even put one brushstroke on to the canvas, he knew exactly what the picture would look like when it was finished. He often used geometry to arrange a picture. He would draw squares and triangles on to his canvas, and fit his figures inside them. Look at the picture of *The Lacemaker* (left), in which Vermeer has used a triangular composition. Can you see the triangle? Its apex is at the top of the woman's head, and its sides slope down to the edges of the picture.

The colours in a Vermeer are golden, rich and mellow. They are comforting colours – none of them startle or upset us. Vermeer realized how important colour is in creating a mood. He knew that certain colours have the power to change our feelings.

Although abstract art is thought of as a modern idea, it has existed for centuries. Many paintings have abstract parts in them even though, often, the artist was not aware of it. Look at the threads spilling out of the sewing box in the picture of *The Lacemaker* (left), for example. The way they tumble and the loose way they are painted is like an abstract painting. If you put a frame around just this area, nobody would guess that it was painted 300 years ago, they would think it was modern. Look for other abstract areas in the paintings in this book.

Pictures with nothing in them

Towards the middle of this century, some modern painters, called abstract artists, began experimenting with colour and shapes. Like Vermeer, they knew about the power of colour, but they took it one step further. They painted pictures that only contained colours and shapes. They had no figures, no landscapes, no objects, nothing recognizable in them at all.

Abstract artists believe that it is possible to affect people's feelings with just colour and form. One of them,

Mark Rothko, painted coloured rectangles with fuzzy edges that appear to float on pools of other, similar colours. Some of the colours and shapes that he used create a feeling of deep calm and peace, others conjure up feelings of tragedy and doom.

Abstract art is about freedom to paint whichever way you want. There are no rules or instructions that tell you how to paint an abstract picture. Some abstract artists have unusual ways of painting. An American called Jackson Pollock dripped paint straight on to the canvas without using a paintbrush. Unlike Seurat and Vermeer, he had no idea what his pictures would be like before he started them. Instead he let them grow, almost by themselves. 'The painting has a life of its own,' he said. 'I try to let it come through.'

◄ *This is an abstract painting. It is called this because it contains no objects, figures or landscapes. Different tones of the same colour have been painted on top of one another. This creates the impression that the colours are floating. Even though it has nothing we recognize in it, this painting can still affect our mood. How do you feel as you look at it?* [Red on Maroon, *Mark Rothko*]

Paint an abstract picture

Abstract paintings consisting of just colours and shapes can fill those who look at them with strong emotions. Try to paint an abstract painting that makes you feel peaceful.

What you need
- paint
- paintbrushes
- paper

What you do

1 Think of two or three colours that you find peaceful. You might like to use cool colours like blue and green, but be careful – they can look cold. Mix in some red and orange to warm them up. Make sure your colours look good with each other. As you are going to paint a peaceful picture, it is important that the colours you choose do not 'fight' each other. Experiment first by mixing different colours and looking at different colour combinations. Paint squares of different colours side by side to see which ones work best.

2 When you have found a combination you like, think of the shapes you are going to paint. What shapes do you think are peaceful? Shapes with curved edges and smooth lines are generally more peaceful than sharp edges and straight lines. Horizontal shapes are more restful than vertical ones.

3 Now paint your shapes in the colours you have chosen. Think of how each shape and each colour affects the one beside it. You may like to leave some areas of white paper, the picture doesn't have to be completely covered with paint.

4 When you have finished, show your picture to a friend. Ask them what feeling they think it shows. Were you successful in creating a feeling of peace? Try to paint another feeling: anger, or love, for example.

5 Fear

Horror stories

Goose bumps, cold shivers, sweaty palms, a horrible feeling of dread. Can you remember the last time you were scared? Did you feel any of these things? Many things make us feel afraid. Some of them are really quite harmless. A fun-fair ride may be terrifying, for example – we feel we are going to be hurt when really we are quite safe. The same is true of films that make us jump in our seats or hide our eyes. Although they terrify us, we know that nothing we see on the screen can really hurt us.

Often it is our own imaginations that make us afraid. We scare ourselves by imagining what is going to happen, what could have happened, or what might have happened to someone else. Scary paintings fill our imaginations with frightening images. The artists want us to feel frightened when we look at them.

Faces of fear

Things that are difficult to understand or are unfamiliar can also be frightening. Monsters and hideous, grotesque faces, for example,

▼ *Everybody in this picture looks scared and alone, yet there is no obvious reason for their fear. Look at the people's faces. Although their expressions are all different, they all seem to experience the same terror. Perhaps they are frightened of each other, or the subway itself, with its maze-like corridors and stairs.* [The Subway, *George Tooker*]

▶ *Carnival masks are usually comical and fun, but the masks in this picture are frightening, especially the one in the middle. This skeleton mask represents death. It is even more scary because it is smiling. What feelings do you think the other masks convey or conceal?*
[Masks and Death, James Ensor]

are scary because we do not come across them normally.

During the Middle Ages, artists carved grotesque stone faces outside churches. They

Grotesque

Nowadays, we use the word 'grotesque' to describe anything that is distorted or exaggerated in an ugly way. This is different from its original meaning. Grotesque comes from the Italian word for a cave or grotto – *grotta*. Grottoes were popular places with the ancient Romans who used either natural ones or man-made ones as places of retreat. Many of these grottoes were decorated with painted panels of fantastic creatures. These creatures were part-human, part-animal and were accompanied by flowers and garlands that covered the walls or ceiling of the grotto. Grotesque creatures became popular again in the sixteenth century, when they were often painted or carved as decorations on houses and furniture.

thought that these horrible monsters would keep evil spirits away. The same thing happened in Africa. Artists there carved wooden masks and figures with twisted, ugly faces to keep them safe from danger.

The first time you look at a painting of a carnival by the modern Belgian artist James Ensor, you think that you are looking at masks. They are horrible, scary masks but it is a picture of a carnival, so it seems quite harmless. Then the real horror starts as you realize that they aren't masks at all but people's faces. What Ensor was trying to show was that everybody has a dark, unpleasant side that is usually kept hidden. In his pictures of grotesque faces, he reveals this side as it really is.

Nightmares

Horrible faces, strange places and peculiar events are the stuff of nightmares. During sleep, the mind can really scare us. It produces images and unfamiliar things that seem quite real at the time.

Several artists have painted the terrifying things that their minds conjured up when they were asleep.

Salvador Dali, a Spanish artist, painted vivid pictures of his dreams. He called them 'hand-painted dream photographs'. His pictures are particularly disturbing because they look as real as photographs, but contain strange things that are never seen in real life.

Henry Fuseli was a Swiss painter who, like James Ensor, explored the darker side of the mind, including dreams and nightmares. His most famous picture, which he painted in 1782, was called *The Nightmare*. It shows a

▼ *This is one of a series of pictures painted by Goya towards the end of his life. It is dark and terrifying. The people and animals are running from the giant who has just snatched up one of them in his huge hands. Everything is menacing and dark. The clouds that loom over the landscape are almost as frightening as the giant himself.* [The Colossus, Francisco José de Goya]

▲ *This painting describes what the artist (the figure with his hands over his ears) felt one day as he was out walking. He felt that nature was screaming at him. He looks terrified and alone. Everything in the picture reflects his mood. The blood-red sky and the lines of the landscape emphasize the sense of horror and fear. [The Scream (1893), Edvard Munch]*

woman in the grip of a terrifying dream. A monstrous demon is sitting on her chest and a wide-eyed horse is bursting through the curtains.

Many of the subjects of paintings by the Spanish artist Goya are straight out of nightmares. He said that 'the sleep of reason produces monsters', and tried to paint the monsters from his own dreams. For most of his life, Goya painted portraits and religious subjects for the Spanish royal family and other wealthy people. Towards the end, however, he retired to a house outside Madrid and decorated its walls with strange, dark pictures. These pictures are of terrifying scenes such as witches dancing crazily at a sabbath, the god Saturn eating one of his children, and a giant striding about scattering people before him.

It was not just the subjects that made Goya's paintings frightening; it was also the way he painted them. He used dark colours and frenzied brushstrokes to create a feeling of terror. Little light penetrates these gloomy landscapes, from which dark and horrifying figures loom.

Feelings of doom

These sinister pictures by Goya were unusual for the time. Until then, artists had mostly painted pictures about stories from the Bible, or from legend or history. Few had painted images from their own minds.

When artists began exploring their own feelings and experiences in order to discover subjects to paint, a

whole new range of pictures appeared. In the nineteenth century, a Norwegian called Edvard Munch based much of his work on his own emotional experiences. He was an unhappy man, and he painted pictures of jealousy, anguish, death and despair. Munch ended his life in a hospital, where he was treated for depression. His anguish was mainly a result of unhappy love affairs. His paintings haunt us because they show the dark, sad side of life that is familiar to everyone to a greater or lesser extent.

At first glance, the paintings of landscapes by Vincent Van Gogh look like straightforward pictures of the French countryside where he lived. Then, as we look closer, we see the way the paint has been applied in thick, swirling brushstrokes. The colours are often strange and disturbing; a dark-blue sky looms over a golden cornfield, for instance. By using these methods, Van Gogh tells us how he felt as he painted.

Van Gogh was poor all his life – he sold only one painting – and troubled by depression and attacks of madness. During one fit, he sliced off part of his ear, and two years later he killed himself with a shotgun. Many of his pictures reflect his anxiety and unhappiness. They are frightening because they are troubled and full of despair.

▲ *When you look at this picture you probably just see a wheatfield with some birds – an attractive landscape. The meaning of the painting changes, though, when you discover that this was the last picture the artist – Van Gogh – painted before he killed himself. Suddenly you see the artist's despair and fear. The sky looks dark and forbidding and the black crows become evil and predatory. It is interesting to see how your opinion of a picture changes the more you learn about it. [Wheatfield with Crows, Vincent Van Gogh]*

Scary shadows

Many people are scared of the dark. There is usually no reason to be scared but our imaginations play tricks with us and create frightening things out of nothing. At night-time, shadows can look terrifying. Often an ordinary thing like a curtain can be transformed into an evil face or a monster by the way the light falls on it. A little cat can look like a big, dangerous lion. It is fun to make a drawing of frightening shadows. Here is how you do it.

What you need
- sticks of charcoal
- paper
- bright light, such as a desk lamp or a torch

What you do

1 Experiment with shining the light on to different objects. Shine the light in a variety of positions, some high, some low, so that it throws big, dramatic shadows on to a wall. Try using a doll, a boot, a sleeping pet, or anything else you can think of.

2 When you have created a really scary-looking shadow, sketch the result in charcoal. Use a big piece of paper and draw with thick strokes to fill all the space.

6 Surprise

The unexpected

It is often thrilling to be surprised – especially by something nice. Sometimes life becomes predictable and boring, nothing exciting or new happens. Then suddenly and unexpectedly, something occurs that shakes us up and makes us look at things in a new way.

Like life, art can also surprise. We get used to paintings and sculpture looking a certain way but then someone comes along and turns the familiar on its head. This person finds a new way of seeing the world, or a new way of painting, and things begin to change.

Most major artists have surprised, even shocked, the public at one time or other. The first paintings by the French Impressionists were dismissed by critics as mere splodges of colour. Now they are among the most popular paintings in the world and cost millions of pounds to buy. Even John Constable, whose paintings of the English countryside look far

from controversial now, shocked his audience when he painted them. They thought his pictures were too realistic and showed too many unpleasant things.

Surprising pictures

As well as surprising us with new ideas, artists also create pictures of surprising things that happen to other people. Because a moment of surprise is very brief, a good way of capturing it accurately is with a camera.

▲ *Many different sorts of surprise are shown on the faces of the people in this picture. A man has come home unexpectedly. He looks tired and shabby. His mother looks astonished to see him. The maid, who has opened the door, looks apprehensive. What do you think his wife and children are feeling?*
[They Did Not Expect Him, *Ilya Repin*]

Photojournalism

The photographer Weegee took pictures of crime and tragedy for the New York daily newspapers. Newspaper pictures often tell a story more effectively than the accompanying words can. Some have become famous because they are such striking images. Sometimes a story is told entirely with pictures. This is called reportage.

During the 1930s and 1940s, the American government paid photographers to record the poverty and hardship of its people. Photographers such as Walker Evans and Dorothea Lange travelled around the poorest areas of the USA. Some of the pictures they took were so disturbing that they shocked the people who saw them. As a result, laws were passed to improve conditions in city slums and in the poor farming communities.

▼ *This woman is suffering from shock. A few minutes earlier, her car had collided with a truck. The policeman is telling her that the driver of the truck is dead. Do you think that newspapers should publish pictures of people at times like this?* [Shock, *Weegee*]

An American newspaper photographer called Weegee had a radio in his car that was tuned into police broadcasts. He heard about accidents and crimes as soon as they happened. He hurried to the scene at once and took dramatic photographs of the people he saw there. The faces of the people in his pictures are frozen forever; startled, distressed, shocked.

Lights, action...

Weegee's photographs show clearly how the human face alters when it is surprised. The eyes widen, the mouth opens, the eyebrows rise.

Look around your home at the things you use every day. Which would you make into a giant sculpture? What materials would you use? Try to see things in a different way, not just as useful objects but as potential works of art. Admire their shape, their decoration, how the light falls on them. You may find that mundane objects are actually quite beautiful.

◀ *This is a scene from the Bible. A banquet held by a king named Belshazzar is interrupted when a hand mysteriously appears and writes four words on the wall. Everybody at the meal is astonished. Rembrandt, who painted this picture, has created a feeling of surprise by showing the figures recoiling from the writing. He has also used lighting to emphasize this; see how the light seems to come from the words (which are written in Hebrew), and how the figures emerge from the shadows.*
[Belshazzar's Feast, Rembrandt van Rijn]

The body also changes: the hands fly up to the face and the body recoils from what it sees. To emphasize what is going on, some artists 'stage' a picture, rather as a director would a play, to create the most dramatic image possible.

One of the greatest 'directors' was the Dutch artist Rembrandt. Like a theatre director, he dressed the cast of his paintings in elaborate, oriental costumes.

He made them express themselves in exaggerated gestures and bathed them in dramatic pools of light.

This is especially evident in his paintings of scenes from the Old Testament. Several of these, such as *The Blinding of Samson* and *Belshazzar's Feast*, show unexpected events. The lighting in these pictures is as important as the figures. It appears as a flash that seems to dazzle the figures.

▲ At first glance this picture looks like a portrait of a grotesque man. But a second look reveals that it is a face made from vegetables. The artist Arcimboldo often painted faces constructed from vegetables, fruit and other everyday things. Apart from surprise, what were your feelings on first seeing the picture?
[Summer, *Giuseppe Arcimboldo*]

Rembrandt was influenced in the way he painted light by an Italian artist, Michelangelo Caravaggio. Both painted pools or shafts of bright light next to areas of shadow or darkness. This dramatic lighting is like a spotlight in the theatre, which shines on to the most important character on the stage.

Like a stage, the dark areas in a painting by Rembrandt or Caravaggio are bigger than the light ones.

This increases the strength and brightness of the pools of light. If the amount of light and dark were equal, the painting would look much less dramatic. The name for the arrangement of the bright and dark areas in a picture is chiaroscuro (from the Italian words for clear – *chiaro* – and obscure – *oscuro*).

Things are not what they seem

When we look at a painting of a surprising event by Rembrandt, we witness the astonishment of the figures in it. When we look at a painting by the Belgian artist René Magritte, we are the ones who are astonished, amused and puzzled.

He painted a picture called *The Use of Words* showing a pipe; below the pipe he wrote 'This is not a pipe.' In his *Portrait of Mr James* he painted a man staring into a mirror. Instead of a reflection of his face, the man sees the back of his head.

Magritte's pictures make us think twice. If that isn't a pipe in that picture, what is it? If a man sees the back of his head in the mirror, what does his face look like?

Soft sculpture

Like the paintings of Magritte, the sculpture of American artist Claes Oldenburg also confuses and surprises. Oldenburg made enormous replicas of everyday objects. Things we take for granted like a typewriter, a hamburger or a drainpipe are enlarged so much that suddenly they are no longer just household objects but sculpture. But these sculptures are not made of marble or bronze like the ones we are used to. They are made of cloth stuffed with foam, which makes them disturbingly soft, like enormous cushions.

Like Magritte, Oldenburg challenges the way we look at things. We are used to sculpture being of 'important' things, such as heroic figures; why should it not be of ordinary, everyday things, too?

Art that uses common-place things in surprising ways is called Pop art. It was particularly popular in America in the 1960s, where artists used images from films, comics and advertising in their work. Roy Lichtenstein, for example, painted enormous pictures that look like comic strips. An

English Pop artist, Richard Hamilton, made collages of images from magazine advertisements. He summed up Pop art as 'popular, transient, expendable, low cost, mass produced, young, witty, sexy, gimmicky, glamorous and big business'. This was quite a new way of looking at art.

▲ *This is a surprising object – a drainpipe made of cloth. Instead of a rigid, shiny pipe it is soft and floppy, like an old pair of jeans.* [Soft Blue Drainpipe, *Claes Oldenburg*]

Soft fruit

Think of a three-dimensional object that is usually hard, such as a box, a telephone or a bowl of fruit and make it into a soft sculpture. Here's how to make the bowl of fruit in the picture.

What you need
- cube of foam about 30 cm on all sides
- sharp knife and an adult to help cut the foam
- scraps of material for the skins of the fruit
- brown or black material for the stalks
- needle and thread to match your material
- kapok for stuffing
- brown felt-tip pen

What you do
1 Ask an adult to hollow out a hole in the centre of the foam and shape the sides of the bowl.

2 Cover the bowl with material. Leave plenty of slack in the hollow and fold the material loosely around the sides and over the edges.

3 Sew the material together under the bowl to keep it together.

4 Get an adult to help you work out the size and shape of the pieces of material you need to make the fruit. Use two pieces for cherries, four for bananas and three or four for apples. Cut the pieces out.

5 Cut out lengths of brown or black material for the stalks.

6 Roll the stalks into thin cylinders, cut them to length and sew each one.

7 Sew the fruit pieces together, leaving a hole for stuffing and for the stalk.

8 Stuff them well, attach the stalks and sew together. The bananas look more realistic with a few brown felt-tip marks on the skin.

Love

Love is...

Songs are sung about it, books are written about it, films are made about it, but what exactly is love? It is the hardest feeling to describe because it takes so many different forms. We can love our family and friends, for example, but this doesn't feel the same as being in love with someone. Then there is the more general kind of love: love of animals, the human race, God, your city (have you ever seen bumper stickers that say 'I love New York'?).

Art is a good way of capturing the different faces of love. It can freeze a moment of tenderness forever. A look of love between two people only lasts a second or two, but in a painting or sculpture it lasts forever.

How to capture love

We have seen how artists use different techniques to show different emotions. These include colour, composition, facial expression, body movement and lighting.

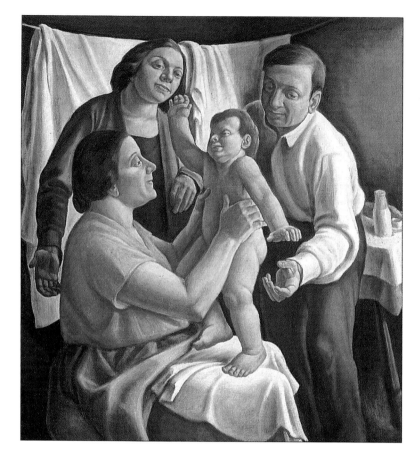

When we look at a picture or a piece of sculpture, there are generally no words accompanying it to help us understand its meaning. The artist has to get his message across without the help of words. In books, or in the cinema, words explain what has happened and what the characters are feeling. In art, what we see has to tell us everything. Often, a picture can say more than words.

▲ *There are three generations of a family in this picture. The parents are showing their first baby to his grandmother. The artist wanted to illustrate the love that can exist between members of the same family. Can you see any physical resemblance between the people in the painting?*
[The First Born, *Daniel R. Celentano*]

Portraits in miniature

In sixteenth-century England, when Queen Elizabeth I was on the throne, many people carried around with them small portraits, called miniatures, of the person they loved. We still do this today, but instead of a painted image, we carry a photograph. Why not paint a miniature of someone special to you?

What you need
- photograph
- watercolours
- paintbrush
- magnifying glass

What you do

1 Find a photograph of the person you are going to paint. One in which you can see their face clearly is best.
2 Cut out a small, circular piece of paper. If you are going to put your miniature in a locket, make sure the paper is the right size and shape to fit inside.

3 Copy the photograph by painting with a fine brush. Use the magnifying glass to help you with the details.
4 If you don't have a locket to put it in, glue the miniature on to a hard piece of card. You could varnish it with clear varnish to protect it from damage and keep it in your pocket.

Feelings are difficult to explain without words, and love is probably the hardest one of all. The usual artistic techniques are not so useful when painting love. Love doesn't suggest any particular colour, for example. It can be a passionate, tranquil or happy feeling. It can even make us feel angry and sad. Therefore, an artist could use red, blue, yellow or any colour at all to paint it.

The same is true of body language. The artist has a wide selection of movement to choose from. Love can be represented by figures dancing, crying, laughing or just lying around dreaming.

Look at the pictures in this chapter and work out what kind of love the figures in each one are experiencing. Is it romantic love, family love or simple affection?

Love stories from the past

Being in love with someone is one of the best feelings in the world. Ever since the first human beings appeared, thousands of years ago, people have been falling in love.

Every country has its own love stories, some of which have existed for centuries. In India, the ancient Hindu book, the *Mahabharata*, contains lots of stories, some of adventure, some of love. One of the greatest love stories is about the god Krishna's love for Radha. Many artists have illustrated this happy story which involves dancing, farming and music. The bright colours, delicate drawing and elegant figures in these pictures all help to create a feeling of pleasure and joyfulness.

The love stories of ancient Greece and Rome were first heard over 2,000 years ago. Sculptors and painters at the time illustrated the stories of the love between gods and godesses such as Hera and Zeus and Psyche and Cupid.

Cupid was the Roman god of love and has been used ever since as a symbol for romance.

These love stories continued to be popular subjects with artists until the eighteenth century.

The Pre-Raphaelites

A group of nineteenth-century English painters called the Pre-Raphaelites also liked to paint love stories from earlier, more romantic times. They found the stories in medieval legends, in the poems of the Italian poet Dante and in the

▼ *Krishna, the figure on the right of this picture, was a Hindu god. His story is told in a book called the* Mahabharata. *Radha was Krishna's great love. In this picture, Krishna is giving her a sacred flower called the lotus. This is a very decorative picture. Look at the colourful, jewelled costumes, the carpet in Radha's house, and the tree.*
[Krishna Presenting a Lotus to Radha]

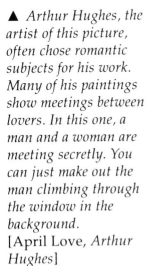

▲ *Arthur Hughes, the artist of this picture, often chose romantic subjects for his work. Many of his paintings show meetings between lovers. In this one, a man and a woman are meeting secretly. You can just make out the man climbing through the window in the background.*
[April Love, *Arthur Hughes*]

plays of William Shakespeare. They do not always have happy endings. Many of Shakespeare's plays are tragedies, including the most famous love story ever, *Romeo and Juliet*, which ends in misunderstanding and death. The Pre-Raphaelite painter John Everett Millais illustrated a scene from another Shakespeare play, *Hamlet*. In this play, Hamlet rejects his girlfriend Ophelia who then goes mad and drowns herself.

Millais' painting shows Ophelia floating down the river, romantically surrounded by flowers. There is sadness in the scene but not the anguish that would be present in real life.

Another Pre-Raphaelite, Arthur Hughes, painted some scenes from legend and others that he made up himself.

Several of these show lovers meeting secretly or on the point of running away together. They do not show the happy, joyful side of love, but the sweet sadness that is felt when obstacles or people come between lovers.

True love

The model for Ophelia by Millias, was a woman named Elizabeth Siddall. She had to lie in a cold bath for hours while Millais painted her. Elizabeth Siddall later became the wife of another Pre-Raphaelite painter, Dante Gabriel Rossetti. Rossetti painted many pictures of his wife. He not only painted her portrait but also used her as a character in his other pictures.

One of his favourite subjects was Dante's poem, *The Divine Comedy*. In it, Dante is accompanied through hell and purgatory to heaven by his girlfriend Beatrix. The love between Dante and Beatrix appealed to Rossetti who saw it as a similar love to the one he had for Elizabeth.

Rossetti painted many sensitive, tender portraits of his wife. These pictures suggest that they were very happy together. However, this is not strictly true. Rossetti was quite cruel to Elizabeth and eventually, feeling ignored and hurt, she killed herself. After her death, Rossetti painted a very moving portrait of her as the character Beatrix.

Many artists have painted and sculpted portraits of the person they love the most. Henri Matisse painted affectionate pictures of his wife, so did Rembrandt, and Marc Chagall painted joyful pictures of himself and his wife on their wedding day.

The names of the lovers in some paintings (for example,

▲ *This picture is about romantic love. The man and woman show their feelings by the way they touch each other. He is kissing her and she holds his hand and puts her arm around his neck. See how realistic their faces and bodies are compared to their clothes. The artist, Gustav Klimt, loved to paint patterns. In this painting the patterns flatten out the bodies and make them decorative. Klimt has used different colours and patterns for the man's and the woman's clothes.*
[The Kiss, *Gustav Klimt*]

▼ *What do you think the mother in this painting is thinking? Her baby is sound asleep, so she doesn't need to be there but she has chosen to sit beside the cradle and watch. Her expression is calm and thoughtful and she holds the cradle's veil lightly in one hand. This is a delicate painting which shows maternal love in a gentle, subtle way.* [The Cradle, *Berthe Morisot*]

The Kiss by Gustav Klimt) and sculptures (such as *The Kiss* by Auguste Rodin) are unknown. But this doesn't matter – the figures are not telling a story and are not portraits. They are showing what love feels like. As they tenderly embrace, they are absorbed in their own feelings – nothing else exists for that moment. The artist has created a closed, intimate world which we can look at but cannot be a part of.

Images of love, especially romantic love, are always popular. Advertisers use them as a means of selling goods. Shoppers identify with attractive, happy people and like to buy goods associated with them. You see lovers on book covers, film posters, holiday brochures and even ice-cream adverts. Look around the shops and see how many images of love you can see. You may be surprised where they turn up.

Family love

A similar, closed world exists in pictures of family groups. Artists such as Mary Cassatt, the modern American artist Daniel R. Celantano and French painter Berthe Morisot have all painted scenes of domestic intimacy and the love shared by members of the same family.

In these pictures the affection between the figures is shown by the way they respond to each other. The artist connects each person to another by means of looks, gestures and body contact. None of the characters look out at us, they are too happy and involved in their own world. This emphasizes the feeling of closeness and love.

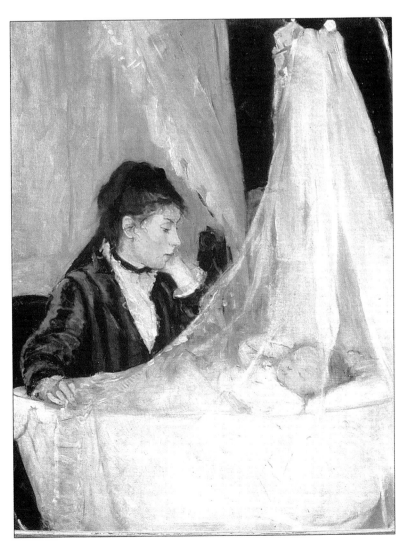

About the artists

ARCIMBOLDO, Giuseppe (1527-1593) An Italian painter, best known for his portrait heads which are made up of human bodies, fruit, vegetables and other everyday items.

BELLOWS, George (1882-1925) This American artist painted realistic pictures of people, landscapes and urban life. He was also a lithographer and illustrated books.

CASSATT, Mary (1845-1926) Although Mary Cassatt was born in America she spent much of her time in Paris where she exhibited with the French Impressionists. She liked to paint pictures of everyday life.

CELENTANO, Daniel R. (1902-) An American artist who paints ordinary people in everyday situations on a large scale.

EL GRECO (1541-1614) A Greek artist, born Domenikos Theotokopoulo in Crete. He spent most of his life in Italy and Spain. His paintings are full of long figures, bright, unusual colours and dramatic lighting.

ENSOR, James (1860-1949) Belgian painter and engraver, famous for his strange paintings which include masked people and fighting skeletons.

GOYA, y Lucientes, Francisco José de (1746-1828) Goya painted the horrors of Napoleon's occupation of Spain as well as portraits and other subjects.

HALS, Frans (c. 1580-1666) A popular Dutch portrait painter whose paintings are full of lively, dashing brushstrokes.

HEARTFIELD, John (1891-1968) This American artist lived in Germany during the time of Hitler. He created photomontages that exposed the evils of war and Nazism.

HUGHES, Arthur (1832-1915) Hughes was one of the last painters to join the English group of artists, the Pre-Raphaelites. His detailed pictures often have a moral.

KLIMT, Gustav (1862-1918) Much of the work of this Austrian artist decorates the inside walls of buildings.

MASACCIO (Tommaso di Giovanni Guidi) (1401-1428) This early Renaissance painter was one of the first to paint human emotions.

MATISSE, Henri (1869-1954) This influential French artist began his career as a lawyer. His pictures include bright colours, simple shapes and patterns, often from oriental sources. Art like his had never been seen before and was very influential.

MOORE, Albert Joseph (1841-1893) This English artist filled his pictures with beautiful people from a lost, golden age.

MORISOT, Berthe (1841-1895) Berthe Morisot was one of the few women Impressionists. She often painted pictures of domestic scenes.

MUNCH, Edvard (1863-1944) This Norwegian painter was very influential, especially in German art. His work is concerned with love and death.

OLDENBURG, Claes (1929-) This Swedish artist, who lives in America, is known for his soft sculptures of enlarged everyday objects.

PICASSO, Pablo (1881-1973) Picasso was one of the most influential artists of the twentieth century. He is best known for his invention, with Georges Braque, of Cubism. This was a way of painting that reduced all objects to geometric forms.

REMBRANDT, Harmensz van Rijn (1606-1669) Rembrandt realized that paint, light and colour are as important as subject matter in a picture. He captured the moods and emotions of his subjects and the rich textures of fabric.

REPIN, Ilya (1844-1930) Most of Repin's paintings are of poor peasants, but he was also a talented portrait and landscape painter. He was a member of a group of Russian artists known as The Wanderers.

RODIN, Auguste (1840-1917) A famous and influential French sculptor, the son of a clerk, who now has two museums devoted to his work, one in Paris and one in Philadelphia.

ROTHKO, Mark (1903-1970) Rothko was born in Russia but lived most of his life in America. His abstract pictures show deep emotions and feelings.

SEURAT, Georges (1859-1891) Seurat was interested in the theory of colour. He invented Pointillism.

SHAHN, Ben (1898-1936) Ben Shahn was born in Russia but settled in America. He liked to paint scenes showing ordinary people.

SHARAKU, Tokhusai All that is known about this Japanese artist is that between 1794 and 1795 he designed 143 prints, mostly of actors.

TOOKER, George (1920-) This American artist uses egg tempera paint in his pictures. Much of his work is about loneliness, fear and despair.

VAN GOGH, Vincent (1853-1890) During his lifetime Van Gogh sold only one picture. He was a teacher and a missionary before he taught himself how to paint. Sadly, he suffered from fits of madness and finally shot himself.

VERMEER, Jan (1632-1675) Although he is famous now, this Dutch painter never sold a painting in his lifetime. His paintings of domestic events have a timeless, still quality.

WEEGEE (Arthur Fellig) (1899-1968) This American photographer listened to police broadcasts on his radio and was always first at the scene of a crime. His photographs appeared in many American newspapers.

Acknowledgements

Academie der Kunste zu Berlin/Ilone Ripke, p.11; Collection of Whitney Museum of American Art, New York, pp.12, 18; Whitney Musem of American Art, New York (photography by Geoffrey Clements, N.Y.), pp.28, 40; Van Gogh Museum, Amsterdam, p.32; Tate Gallery, London, p.43; Tate Gallery, London/Copyright © Claes Oldenburg, p.38; © Weegee/Magnum Photos, New York, p.35.

All other pictures are from the Bridgeman Art Library, courtesy of the following organizations: British Museum, London, p.4; Hermitage, St Petersburg/© Matisse, Succession H. Matisse/DACS 1994, p.5; Wallace Collection, London, p.7; The Metropolitan Museum of Art, from the Collection of James Stillman, Gift of Dr Ernest G. Stillman, 1922 (22.16.17), p.8; British Library, London, p.10 and *cover*; National Gallery, London, pp.13, 36; Christie's, London, p.16; Tate Gallery/© DACS 1994 p.17; © DACS 1994, p.29; Brancacci Chapel, Santa Maria del Carmine, Florence, p.20; Birmingham City Museums and Art Gallery, p.22; Art Institute of Chicago, USA, p.23; Louvre, Paris, p.24; the Louvre Paris/ Giraudon, p.37; Tate Gallery London/© Kate Rothko-Prizel & Christopher Rothko/ARS, New York, p.26; Musée des Beaux Arts, Liege, p.29; Prado, Madrid, p.30; Nasjonalgalleriet, Oslo/© Munch Museum/ Munch Estate/ BONO, Oslo and DACS, London 1994, p.31; Tretyakof Gallery, Moscow, p.34; the Board of Trustees of the Victoria and Albert Museum, London, p.42; Osterreichisches Galerie, Vienna, p.44; Musée d'Orsay, Paris/ Giraudon, p.45.

All the illustrations are by Celia Chester. The photographs on p.39 are by Zul Mukhida.

If copyright in any picture reproduced in this book has unwittingly been infringed, Touchstone Publishing Ltd apologizes and will pay an appropriate fee to the rightful owner as if we had been able to obtain prior permission.

Index